Moon Days

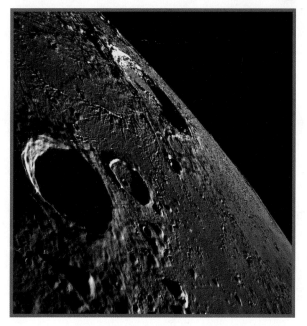

by Eva Liebson
illustrated by Kenneth Batelman

Harcourt

Orlando   Boston   Dallas   Chicago   San Diego

Visit *The Learning Site!*

www.harcourtschool.com

The sky at night is beautiful. It is full of things we haven't always understood. It is very, very dark. It is covered with bright stars.

People have looked up at the night sky for centuries. They have looked up at the moon and wondered what it is.

The moon is not a star. It is a cold ball of rock. It orbits our planet, Earth, moving around it. The moon is Earth's satellite.

The moon shines in the night sky, but it makes no light of its own. Instead, it reflects the light of the sun. The sun shines on the moon, lighting up the moon's surface. The sun's light makes the moon glow white, yellow, or sometimes orange. We can see the moon because the sun's light makes it shine.

From Earth we can see large dark spots on the moon's surface. Some people think that these dark spots look like a face. They refer to these spots as "the man on the moon."

These dark spots on the moon are large craters. Craters form when an object in space crashes into the surface of the moon, making a hole.

Craters on the moon can be very large and deep. The crater Copernicus is 56 miles across and 9,500 feet deep.

The moon's surface also has seas, but the moon's seas don't have any water. They are flat plains. Astronauts landed in the Sea of Tranquillity in 1969. It is 650 miles across.

The picture on page 4 shows one side of the moon. This is the side we see all the time.

The picture on this page shows the other side of the moon. It is called the moon's dark side. It looks very different from the side we see. The dark side doesn't have any large seas. We never see the moon's dark side from Earth.

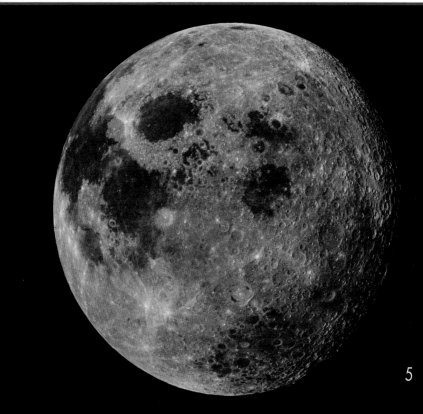

Earth moves around in space, and the moon does, too. Earth and the moon both move in two ways. One movement is called rotation. Earth and the moon both rotate, or spin around on an axis.

Imagine Earth in space. Earth spins around, or rotates, in space. The axis runs from the North Pole to the South Pole. Earth spins around this imagined center line.

Earth completes one spin, or rotation, every twenty-four hours. That is why one day is twenty-four hours long. As Earth rotates, different parts of Earth have day, and different parts have night.

The moon also rotates around its axis. It completes one spin every twenty-seven and a half days.

The second way Earth and the moon move is called revolution. Earth revolves around the sun, moving in a circle around it. The moon revolves around Earth.

It takes the moon twenty-seven and a half days to revolve around Earth. That's the same amount of time as one of its rotations. That is why we always see the same side of the moon.

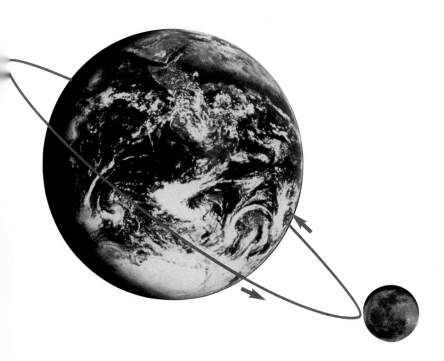

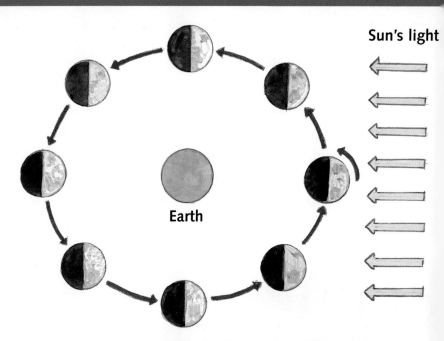

Sun's light

Earth

The moon we see doesn't always look like it has the same shape. Sometimes it is round. Sometimes it is half of a circle. Sometimes it looks like the letter C. The moon appears to change shape as it moves around Earth.

The moon doesn't really change shape. What changes is the part of the moon that is lit by the sun's light. As the moon moves around Earth, the sun lights up different parts of it. When we can't see the moon at all, the sun is shining on the side of the moon that we can't see.

When the moon looks like a complete circle, the sun is shining on the side of the moon that we can see. The diagram below shows how the sun lights up different parts of the moon.

The different shapes of the moon are called the moon's phases. Long ago, people used to mark the passing of time according to the phases of the moon.

The moon we can't see is called the new moon. When this happens, the moon is between Earth and the sun. The sun shines on the moon's other side. As the moon continues its orbit, we slowly see more of it. First, we see a crescent moon. Then, we see a half circle. Next, we see a gibbous moon. Finally, we see a full moon.

As the moon continues its orbit, it appears smaller. After the full moon, we see a gibbous moon, then a half circle, then a crescent moon. When we see no moon again, the moon's orbit has come back to where it started.

Sometimes Earth moves directly between the moon and the sun. The moon is in Earth's shadow in space. This is an eclipse of the moon, or a lunar eclipse. During a lunar eclipse, the moon appears orange. That's because the sun's light passes through Earth's atmosphere before it reaches the moon.

Sometimes the moon moves directly between the sun and Earth. It blocks the sun's light. For a few minutes on Earth, the light dims. This is an eclipse of the sun, or a solar eclipse.

In the photograph below, the moon is the black object. It is moving in front of the white sun.

The moon also affects the level of the water on Earth. This movement of the water is called the tide. When the tide is high, the water level is high. When the tide is low, the water level is low.

People at the beach can watch the tide get lower and higher. When the tide is low, the water seems far away. As the tide begins to rise, the water gets closer and closer.

Why does the tide rise and fall? The moon causes it.

Gravity is a force that causes things to move toward a very large object, such as a planet or a satellite. The moon doesn't have much gravity, but that little bit causes the tides on Earth.

As Earth spins on its axis, different places on Earth have the moon overhead. When the moon is overhead, these places have high tide. The moon's gravity pulls the water toward it. This makes the water level rise. The places on the other side of Earth also have high tide.

When the moon is not overhead, the tide is low.

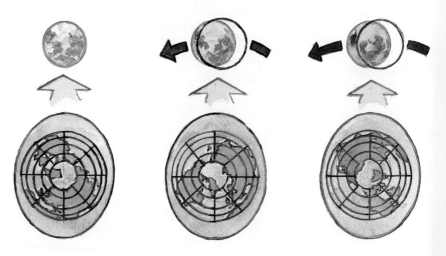

People always have been interested in the moon. Early people weren't sure what the moon was. They weren't sure how Earth moved in space. They didn't understand that Earth moved around the sun and the moon moved around Earth.

Later, telescopes were invented. Scientists learned new things about the moon's surface. They learned how the moon moves in space.

But they still wondered what the moon was really like. The only way to find out was to travel to the moon.

People tried many ideas to get to the moon. In 1961 Yury Gagarin, a pilot from the Soviet Union, was the first person to travel into space.

Less than a month later, Alan Shepard was the first American to travel into space.

Then on July 20, 1969, Neil Armstrong and Edwin "Buzz" Aldrin landed on the moon. Armstrong made the first human footprint on the moon.

tongs used to pick up lunar samples

moon rock, Breccia

moon rock, Olivene

Aldrin was right behind him. They bounced on the moon's surface because the moon has very little gravity. They saw what Earth looks like from the moon's surface. They collected moon rocks.

American astronauts landed on the moon five more times. The astronauts studied the different seas and craters. They saw moon mountains and valleys. They brought back more moon rocks for scientists on Earth to study. They even rode around in a moon buggy.

It was hard for people on Earth to imagine that someone was walking and jumping on the moon. The astronauts sent pictures back to Earth, but it was still hard to imagine what the moon was like.

No one has set foot on the moon since 1972. But someday, people will go again. Right now, we can see the moon from Earth. And we can still wonder.